GREAT EXPLORATIONS

ROBERT E. PEARY

To the Top of the World

PATRICIA CALVERT

BENCHMARK BOOKS

MARSHALL CAVENDISH
NEW YORK

For my father,
Edgar C. Dunlap,
who explored the world he lived in

With special thanks to Stephen Pitti, Yale University,
for his careful reading of this manuscript.

Benchmark Books
Marshall Cavendish Corporation
99 White Plains Road
Tarrytown, New York 10591-9001

Copyright © 2002 by Marshall Cavendish Corporation
Map by Rodica Prato
All rights reserved.
No part of this book may be reproduced in any form without written permission of the publisher.

Library of Congress Cataloging-in-Publication Data
Calvert, Patricia
Robert E. Peary: To the Top of the World
p. cm.—(Great explorations)
Includes bibliographical references (p.).
ISBN 0-7614-1242-5
1. Peary, Robert E. (Robert Edwin), 1856-1920—Journeys—Arctic regions—Juvenile literature.
2. Explorers—United States—Biography—Juvenile literature. 3. North Pole—Juvenile literature. [1. Peary, Robert E.
(Robert Edwin), 1856-1920. 2. Explorers. 3. North Pole—Discovery and exploration.] I. Title. II. Series.
G635.P4 C35 2001   919.804'092—dc21   00-051900

Photo Research by Candlepants Incorporated
Cover Photo and Insert : Corbis
The photographs in this book are used by permission and through the courtesy of; *Corbis* : 12, 24, 41; Michael
Prince, title page; Galen Rowell, 6, 32; Bettmann, 9, 11, 25, 27, 52, 57, 64; Kennan Ward, 36; Hulton Deutsch
Collection, 68. *General Research Division*, *The New York Public Library*, *Astor Lenox and Tilden Foundations* :
15, 18, 23, 30, 33, 35, 38, 43, 45, 49, 51, 58, 59, 60, 63.

Printed in Hong Kong
1   3   5   6   4   2

Contents

The compass, with which men have explored unknown regions of the globe, proved to be useless close to the North Pole. It pointed to the <u>magnetic pole</u>, not the spot at the top of the world.

foreword

The North Pole is the point where an imaginary line drawn through the earth, representing its axis, would exit the earth's surface at the top of the world. The South Pole is the point where the same imaginary line would exit at the opposite end of the globe.

That dot at the top of the world is more than 400 miles (650 kilometers) from land. Beneath the ten-foot-thick ice cap covering the Pole, the Arctic Ocean is five miles (eight kilometers) deep. A permanent marker can't be placed at the Pole to tell other explorers where it's located, because the polar ice shifts constantly with the movement of the sea below. No landmarks identify the Pole so that travelers can recognize it.

Yet the lure of the frozen North has occupied the imaginations of adventurers since long before the day of modern explorers. Perhaps we should not be surprised that humanity's quest for the Pole sometimes ended in mutiny, madness—and even murder.

THE MAGNETIC POLE

The needle on a compass points to the magnetic pole, not to the North Pole at the top of the world. Like its famous cousin, the magnetic pole also is an invisible dot on the globe, but it lies 965 miles (1,556 kilometers) south of the North Pole, off the coast of Bathurst Island in the Arctic Ocean. It was discovered in 1831 by Scottish explorer James Clark Ross and now belongs to Canada. For reasons scientists can't yet explain, it shifts a little each year. When Ross first found it, the magnetic pole was 465 (748 kilometers) miles farther south than it is today.

At the North Pole, the Arctic Ocean is covered with an ice cap ten feet thick. The ice shifts constantly, due to the movement of the sea beneath it; therefore, a permanent marker can't be placed at the Pole to tell other travelers where it's located.

O N E

The North Pole— Before Peary

Wee saw the first Ice, which we wondered at . . .
thinking it had beene white Swannes
—A Dutch sailor, 1596

Pytheas, a sailor from the Greek colony of Massilia (the modern-day city of Marseilles, France), set out in 320 B.C. to search for deposits of tin located in unknown northern lands. On his return, he told of a place where the sun lit the sky at midnight and the seas were "curdled" by ice. People believed Pytheas was lying or mad.

In A.D. 984, the Norse chieftain Eric the Red—exiled from Iceland for murder—gathered his defenders together and sailed west aboard twenty-five *knarr*, or small merchant ships. They settled along the east coast of Greenland, where they came upon the Inuits, an Eskimo tribe whose name means "the real people." These dark-skinned people lived

Eric the Red was exiled from Iceland for murder. With his defenders,
he sailed away and settled along the east coast of Greenland.

in such poverty that the Norsemen called them *skraelings*, "the wretched ones."

Whalers from Spain and Portugal had made their way into the arctic waters by 1372. Soon traders from Spain and Portugal were dreaming of a passage over the top of the world to India and China, known since Marco Polo's day to be rich in silks, spices, and perfumes. English and Dutch whalers plundered the northern seas for bowhead whales that measured up to seventy feet (twenty meters) in length, and yielded as much as forty to fifty tons (forty-five metric tons) of valuable oil. In 1587, John Davis rounded the southern tip of Greenland, establishing a "farthest-north" record for England of 72° N., and his name was given to the strait between Greenland and Baffin Island. In 1596, Willem Barents established a new record of 76° N. for Holland.

Between 1607 and 1611, English explorer Henry Hudson, for whom New York's Hudson River and Canada's Hudson Bay are named, tried, on four voyages, to find a passage to the Far East by way of either the northeast or the northwest. On his first voyage, he reached 80° N., a record that held for 165 years.

The Royal Society of London sent Commodore Constantine Phipps on a mission over the Pole to Asia in 1773. It failed, but a fourteen-year-old boy on board, Horatio Nelson, earned his sea legs on the voyage. As Lord Nelson, he later defeated Napoleon at the Battle of Trafalgar.

William Edward Parry of the British Royal Navy was the first explorer to try "manhauling" his way to the North Pole. In 1827, he set off across the ice with twenty-five men and two heavy sledge-boats fitted with iron runners. As the sledges were dragged toward the Pole, Parry discovered that the drift of the ice carried his expedition southward almost as fast as the men struggled north. Even so, Parry set a new record for England of 82° 45' N. The continuing search for a Northwest Passage resulted in an expedition in 1845 led by Sir John Franklin,

English explorer Henry Hudson made four voyages into the Arctic, hoping to find a route to Asia. His men finally mutinied and set Hudson adrift, and he was never seen again.

who commanded the ships *Erebus* and *Terror*. Terror, indeed, is what befell both crews after their vessels were trapped in the ice; every man perished. In 1859, the bones of two members from the Franklin expedition were discovered on the beach of King William Island, Canada.

Henry Grinnell, an American merchant, funded an expedition in 1850 to find Franklin. The ship's surgeon, Dr. Elisha Kent Kane, went on to lead a second expedition in 1853 and was the first white explorer to

Dr. Elisha Kane published Arctic Explorations, which described voyages he'd made to the Arctic in 1856.

live with the Eskimos. Dr. Kane was also a skillful writer who made arctic adventure magical for ordinary readers. In 1862, a children's Sunday school paper published a report of his exploits, along with one of his pen-and-ink sketches.

Charles Francis Hall followed Kane's example of living with the

Inuits. He learned to eat raw seal meat, wear Eskimo fur-and-leather clothing, and died in the Arctic in 1871, reportedly poisoned by his own men. The British, alarmed by the achievements of the Americans and the explorations of Baron Nordenskjold of Sweden, sent Captain George Nares to the Arctic to reclaim the farthest-north record for the Crown. A new record was indeed set—83° N.

As the nineteenth century came to a close, the prospect of locating what was called "the white grail" inspired adventurers from Scandinavia, Britain, Germany, Austria, Russia, and the United States to be first to reach the North Pole. The stage was set for the right moment and the right man to meet. In April 1909, they did.

SEARCHING FOR THE GRAIL

In medieval legend, the Holy Grail was the cup Jesus drank from at the Last Supper. Twelfth-century French writers developed the idea of a grail as a sacramental symbol that could be possessed only by men who were pure of heart. In the English tales of King Arthur, Sir Galahad, the noblest knight of the Round Table, was one of only a few men to be successful in his quest for the Grail.

In modern times, to say that someone "searches for the grail" means that he or she is on a quest for something very difficult to find.

T W O

When Dreams Begin

I don't want to live and die without accomplishing anything or without being known beyond a narrow circle of friends.
        —Robert E. Peary, 1880, from a letter to his mother

Robert Edwin Peary was born in Cresson, Pennsylvania, on May 6, to a family of businessmen, not explorers or adventurers. His father, Charles Nutter Peary, had moved from Maine to the mountains of Pennsylvania to join his brothers in the shook trade, or the manufacture of barrel staves.

Charles Peary insisted—as his son would later—that the proper pronunciation of the family name rhymed with *weary*, explaining that it was an Americanized version of the French name Pierre. Less than three years after the birth of his only child, Charles Peary died of pneumonia. The boy's mother, the former Mary Wiley, wasn't left penniless.

Robert Edwin Peary—called Bertie by his mother—was full of mischief, which included pegging rocks through windows. Yet there was always something shy and thoughtful about the boy.

She inherited $12,000 (about $210,000 in current dollars) from her husband's portion of the shook business, and returned to her own family near Portland, Maine.

Mary Peary never remarried. Instead, she devoted her attention to her son, a fair-skinned, blue-eyed, reddish-haired boy she fondly called Bertie. That nickname embarrassed him, and he preferred to be called Bert.

His mother's affection was both a blessing and a burden to the fatherless boy. Because Bert was shy, sensitive, and spoke with a slight lisp, Mrs. Peary treated him more like a daughter than a son. She taught him needlework, reminded him that he wasn't as strong as other children, and sent him out to play in a bonnet to protect him from the sun.

Not surprisingly, Bert was harassed by other boys. He got into fist-fights to prove he wasn't a sissy, and he often came home bruised and disheveled. Mrs. Peary was shocked that Bert's other acts of rebellion included pegging rocks through barn windows to hear the glass "jingle." He even tried to trip old Mr. Wiley, just to see what would happen if his grandfather took a tumble.

Mrs. Peary enrolled Bert in Sunday school when he was six, hoping to improve his behavior. In a March 22, 1862, issue of the *Sunday School Advocate*, the boy saw an article that fired his curiosity. Since he couldn't read on his own, he begged his mother to read it to him over and over.

The article reported the explorations of Dr. Elisha Kent Kane, who'd made two trips to the frozen North and written about them in *Arctic Explorations*, published in 1857. Bert eagerly studied an accompanying sketch, drawn by Dr. Kane himself, of Eskimo boys playing a game like baseball.

The coast of Maine, where Bert and his mother settled, was a wonderful place for a boy to grow up. Bert hiked, fished, collected birds' eggs, and explored the heavily wooded islands in Casco Bay. He was enchanted by Eagle Island, seventeen acres in size, and vowed to own it someday. By the time he entered high school in Portland at fourteen, Bert had became an expert taxidermist and was asked to give a presentation at the Portland Museum of Natural History.

Upon graduation in 1873, Bert was awarded a scholarship to Bowdoin College in Brunswick, Maine. Nearly fifty years earlier, Nathaniel Hawthorne and Henry Wadsworth Longfellow had graduated from the same college. In order to help finance his education, Bert sold his collection of stuffed birds and animals.

The college was only twenty-three miles from home, but Mrs. Peary refused to be parted from her son, and accompanied him to Bowdoin.

Twenty-first-century boys would object if their mothers went to college with them, but Bert—though he sometimes resented his mother's possessiveness—depended on her unfailing support and encouragement.

Bert entered a civil engineering program, which prepared young men for careers as builders of bridges, canals, piers, and roads. He was still rather shy, but he earned a reputation around Bowdoin as a "brilliant" student. Yet a former classmate recalled, "he seemed to be by himself, going on long tramps, hunting and fishing. . . . I never heard of him forming any particular friendships."

Bert studied hard, noting in his diary that he often worked from five in the morning until eight at night. Soon he attracted the attention of one of his professors, George Leonard Vose. In an after-class gab session, Vose speculated on how a man might get to the North Pole. He suggested that the problem earlier explorers had experienced with supply lines could be solved by establishing caches of food and provisions along the way *before* making a dash for the Pole. It was an idea Bert Peary never forgot.

In 1876, when he was twenty years old, Bert attended the Centennial Exposition in Philadelphia, where he enjoyed the exhibits from faraway countries. He admitted that he was glad to have been born at the time in history that he was. If he'd come into the world later, "every spot will have felt the pressure of man's foot." How could he experience true adventure if he walked only where other men had already trod?

Bert confessed his thoughts to Mary Kilby, a girl from Portland he'd grown fond of while in high school. He told her that he couldn't understand why Maine farmers lived out their lives in the same place, doing the same things their fathers and grandfathers had done.

After graduating second in a class of fifty-one and being elected to Phi Beta Kappa, Bert moved with his mother to Fryeburg, Maine, near the New Hampshire border. The young engineer practiced his surveying

After he entered Bowdoin College in Brunswick, Maine, young Peary earned a reputation as a "brilliant" student, but some students noted that he kept mostly to himself.

skills and was appointed justice of the peace in 1878. When he found no employment as a surveyor, Bert decided to map the town to keep himself busy.

About the time his survey was finished, Bert read a notice on a bulletin board at the Fryeburg post office. Draftsmen were wanted by the U.S. Coast and Geodetic Survey office in Washington, D.C.; ten dollars per week was offered for a six-month trial period. Bert applied, telling no one for fear he'd be turned down. He enclosed his map of Fryeburg as an example of the work he could do.

Bert's application was accepted, and he left home for his new job on July 4, 1879. It was Independence Day in more ways than one: this time, Mother didn't go with him!

Although he'd been desperate to get the job, no sooner did he have it than he longed to be free to tramp the woods and fields as he used to do. His desire to be free also led him to break his recent engagement to Mary Kilby. The idea of getting married now seemed like a bad dream.

When his trial period at the government office was over, Bert was hired for a permanent position at a salary of forty dollars a month. With his new wealth he fulfilled a vow he'd made to himself when only a boy: he purchased Eagle Island for his own.

Again, Peary grew restless. Working all day in a stuffy office wasn't how he wanted to live. He was twenty-four years old and expected to do great things. He asked himself, "What have I done? . . . I wish to acquire a name which shall . . . make me feel that I am peer to anyone I may meet." When he learned that the U.S. Navy had openings for civil engineers, he didn't hesitate before applying. He studied hard for the examination, and two months later was notified that he'd gotten an appointment.

In October 1880, Bert explained his aspirations to his mother. "Many men have made themselves world-famous," he wrote, "by looking forward to something sure to be of importance in the future, making the subject thoroughly their own, and then when the right moment came stepping forward as the chief and only authority."

Bert Peary longed to find a subject to call his own, to become expert at something that would lift him above ordinary men. He'd composed a poem for his graduating class at Bowdoin; one of its lines read, "Give me the restless wild essence of life." The wild essence of life was what the tall, shy young man from Portland, Maine, longed to experience firsthand.

THREE

My Name before the World

I never for a moment doubted that I should Succeed.
—Robert E. Peary, 1886, on his first trip to Greenland

Engineers who entered the U.S. Navy from civilian life were looked down upon by men of the "regular" navy. Nevertheless, Bert was pleased to be addressed as Lieutenant Peary and thought he looked impressive in his new uniform.

Peary's first important assignment was the construction of a pier to replace a dilapidated one at the U.S. naval station at Key West in 1882. In spite of getting malaria soon after he arrived in Florida, the twenty-six-year-old lieutenant carefully studied all the maps, charts, and reports available regarding the job. After a disagreement with the commander in charge of the project—an Annapolis man who resented suggestions from a non-navy whippersnapper—Peary was asked to take over. He completed the pier on time and saved the Navy three thousand dollars.

Two years later, Peary assisted in a survey for a proposed canal route across Nicaragua. As always, Bert prepared himself with care. He studied everything he could about the country—its geography, the language and customs of its people, and its plant and animal life. The survey took three months and required sloshing through wet, snake-infested jungles, but shortened the canal by sixteen miles (twenty-six kilometers), a potential savings for the U.S. government of $17 million.

After returning to Washington, Bert spent a few hours browsing through a secondhand bookstore, a favorite pastime. He found a pamphlet by a Swedish explorer, Baron A. E. Nordenskjold, recounting his travels into the little-known interior of Greenland. The young man's dreams of northern adventures were rekindled; soon he was reading everything he could find about arctic exploration. Six months later, Peary declared, "The time has arrived now for an entire change in the expeditionary organization of Arctic research parties."

Just as he'd earlier taken the initiative when surveying the village of Fryeburg, Peary plotted a route over Greenland's ice cap, a frozen wasteland that stretched 1,500 (2,414 kilometers) miles east to west across the northern part of the country and 900 (1,448 kilometers) miles north to south.

Of course, such an adventure required time and money. Bert requested a six-month leave of absence from the navy and borrowed five hundred dollars from his mother, who was not pleased by his scheme. In May 1886, he left Washington and headed—alone—to Newfoundland. From there he took a whaler, the *Eagle*, to Greenland. He told his mother that he was "impatient to reach that northern region which holds my future name."

At Ritenbenk, Greenland, Peary met the young Danish vice-governor, Christian Maigaard, who was intrigued by the plan Peary confided to him. Maigaard warned Bert about the perils of going inland alone and insisted on accompanying him. In June 1886, the two men began their journey, each pulling a lightweight sled made of animal hides, hickory, and steel. Maigaard almost perished when he broke through a snow bridge above a deep crevasse; later, he fell into a glacier pond and nearly drowned.

Such hazards couldn't force the two explorers back to Ritenbenk after their one-hundred-mile excursion into the interior—but a dangerous shortage of food did. Peary's first trip to the Arctic taught him that proper provisions would be essential to the success of any future venture.

On his return to Washington, Peary published a report of his journey, which earned him election to the prestigious American Society for the Advancement of Science. He was determined to build on what he'd accomplished, and he told his mother the trip had "brought my name before the world." Bert was sure the next trip—he was already planning it—would bring him even more acclaim. He'd found a subject to call his own; it consumed him from that moment on.

As an only son, however, Bert knew how much his mother depended on him, and he urged her to remember, "I *must* have fame & cannot reconcile myself to years of commonplace drudgery." The italics were his, and revealed his passion not only for the Arctic but for acclaim. Mary Peary viewed the matter differently. "Such fame is dearly bought," she warned.

Peary's next job wasn't in the Arctic, however. It was a second trip to Nicaragua, where he took charge of a project to continue the canal survey for the Maritime Canal Company. This time he was accompanied by a personal servant, Matthew Henson, whom he'd recently hired. Henson, a black man ten years younger than Peary, was also a seeker of adventure. He'd shipped to China aboard the *Katie Hines* as a cabin boy when he was only twelve, and later spent four years as a crewman on ships to Japan, the Phillipines, North Africa, and Russia.

Matthew Henson (standing behind Peary) had gone to sea when he was only twelve years old. Peary hired him as a valet, but Henson, who accompanied the explorer on all his arctic expeditions, became much more than that.

The second Nicaragua survey took seven months, giving Peary time to consider a marriage proposal he'd made to pretty Josephine Diebitsch. Bert was still wary of tying himself down, but he decided that "Jo" wasn't the kind of woman who'd hamper his ambitions. When he returned from Nicarauga in 1888, the couple were married, and-—just as she'd gone off to college with him—Bert's mother accompanied her son on his honeymoon!

Peary hoped the second Nicaragua survey would add luster to his reputation; instead, the canal project was put on hold after Congress cut appropriations for it. Peary turned his attention again to Arctic exploration, but only six weeks after his wedding, he was stunned to learn that a Norwegian zoology professor, Fridtjof Nansen, and five companions had skied across the Greenland ice cap at its narrow southern end. Nansen's career on the ice had begun when he was only

Robert Peary married Josephine Diebitsch in 1888. He believed she wouldn't interfere with his arctic explorations. He was right. "Jo" went to the Arctic with him and endured many of the same hardships he did.

FRIDTJOF NANSEN

Fridtjof Nansen was the first to cross the Greenland ice cap. Robert Peary envied Nansen's success, and when the Norwegian wrote about his journey, Peary called the book "pretentious."

twenty-one and worked on a sealing ship in Greenland's waters. Nansen, too, dreamed of reaching the Pole.

But Bert Peary, now thirty-two years old, had become possessive of the Arctic. No man could "own" the Pole, yet he felt it belonged to *him.* Bert believed Nansen had tried to upstage him in the eyes of the world, and after reading the Norwegian's book about his journey, he called it "a pretentious affair."

Peary's desire for fame often made him a poor loser. By contrast, polar historians regard Nansen as a man of distinction on several levels. He was awarded the Nobel Peace Prize in 1922 for his work with prisoners after World War I, and to the end of his life he supported the efforts of other men to explore both the North and South Poles.

Although he was disappointed by the attention paid to Nansen's journey, Peary nurtured his dreams by continuing to read about and study the Arctic. He appealed to various organizations to help finance a more ambitious trip than the one with Maigaard but was turned down each time. An invitation to speak at the Brooklyn Institute about his first Greenland trip briefly lifted his spirits.

Finally, in the winter of 1890, nearly ten thousand dollars for another expedition was raised through the efforts of the American Geographical Society, the Brooklyn Institute, and the Philadelphia Academy of Natural Sciences. Peary insisted that the exploration party be kept small—ideally, no more than six members—because he believed a small group was "absolutely essential to success." He planned to use sledges pulled by dogs, as the Eskimos did, rather than by men, as Parry had tried in 1827. He was firm about another point: the group must have only one leader—Robert E. Peary.

Newspaper accounts of the expedition prompted young men around the world to offer their services, and Peary was able to select his team from among many applicants.

In spite of his small stature, twenty-five-year-old John Verhoeff, a former Yale student, was selected. (Verhoeff contributed two thousand dollars to the expedition, making him an attractive choice.) Langdon Gibson, brother of well-known artist Charles Dana Gibson, had no money but was a tall, strong, experienced outdoorsman and a member of the American Ornithologist Society. Eivind Astrup, of Norway, was selected; Matthew Henson, Peary's personal servant, was automatically included. A choice that astonished everyone was Peary's wife, Jo.

Properly planned, such a journey required the services of a physician. Dr. Frederick Albert Cook, who had recently lost his wife and new-born daughter in childbirth, was searching for a way to recover from

Jo

Peary met Josephine Diebitsch in 1882 at Marini's, a dancing club in Washington, D.C. She was the daughter of a scholar connected with the Smithsonian Institution and assisted him as a librarian. She also was stylish and vivacious. Having met Jo, Bert couldn't forget her, and when he made his first trip to Greenland in 1886, he named his sledge the *Sweetheart* with her in mind.

"I cannot but admire her courage," Peary wrote in the preface of *My Arctic Journal*, his wife's account of her first trip to the Arctic. Jo Peary, who had been accustomed to the most civilized kind of life, learned to hunt, to hike long distances in subzero weather, and to dress in traditional native garb. She came to respect the Inuits, whom she undiplomatically called "the queerest, dirtiest-looking individuals" she had ever seen. She concluded her journal by musing, "What the future will bring . . . no one can tell."

Josephine (Jo) Peary had always been accustomed to the finer things in life, yet she fully supported her husband's quest for the North Pole. "I cannot but admire her courage," wrote her husband.

his grief. When he read a report of Peary's expedition in the New York *Telegram*, Cook noted that a final decision about applicants had not been made. Cook wrote to Peary, was interviewed, and became the seventh member of the team.

Born in Hortonville, New York, in 1865, the same year the Civil War ended, Cook was nine years younger than Peary. There were similarities between the two men that were almost eerie: Peary's father died before Bert was three years old; Cook's father died when Fred was five. Cook's widowed mother raised her "Freddy" alone, as Peary's widowed mother raised her "Bertie" alone.

In childhood, each boy was a lover of nature and spent hours tramping through woods and fields. Each boy spoke with a slight lisp; each boy engaged in fistfights to prove he wasn't a sissy. Each boy believed he could succeed at whatever he tackled by diligence and hard work.

Most amazing of all, both Cook and Peary had been stirred by the arctic tales of Dr. Kane. As a result, Dr. Frederick A. Cook was to play a more dramatic role in the life of Robert E. Peary than either man could have guessed at their meeting in 1891.

f O U R

A World of Ice: Magic and Madness

It seems almost sure my dream of years is ended . . . have been traveling over the roughest kind of ice and ground . . . in bitterness of spirit.

—*Robert E. Peary, 1892, from Greenland's ice cap*

At 5:00 P.M. on June 6, 1891, the North Greenland Expedition sailed from Brooklyn aboard a 280-ton (250-metric-ton) sealing ship, the *Kite*. Also on board were nine professors from the Philadelphia Academy of Natural Sciences, who planned to winter farther down the Greenland coast after Peary's group was dropped off to the north.

As the *Kite* moved toward Newfoundland and Labrador, the ship was halted by ice for hours at a time. On June 23, just as Captain Pike found a path through a bad stretch, a gale came up with high winds and cold rain, stalling progress again. When Godhavn, on the west coast of Greenland, loomed into view, it was greeted with cheers by the explorers.

Except for bad weather and bouts of seasickness, the journey had been a safe one. That changed on July 11. Peary and Jo had gone on deck to watch how the *Kite* plowed through the soft, or "rotten," ice. The ship's rudder suddenly struck a huge chunk, slamming the tiller against the wheelhouse where Peary was standing. His right leg was snapped, just above the ankle.

Dr. Cook splinted the leg (the break was clean and didn't need to be set), then treated Peary's pain with whiskey and morphine. The

The <u>Kite</u> was hampered by ice many times on its way to the coast of Greenland. On July 11, 1891, as it plowed through a patch of "rotten" ice, the tiller slammed against the wheelhouse where Peary was standing, breaking his ankle.

expedition Peary hoped to begin needed an able-bodied leader; if he'd been made of different stuff, he might have given up then and there.

When the *Kite* ran into more ice that had to be dynamited out of the ship's path, however, Professor Angelo Heilprin, leader of the scientists' group, decided the whole adventure was too dangerous. He told Mrs. Peary that it was her duty to take her husband home. Jo, who knew what the journey meant to Bert, kept silent.

In late July, the *Kite* passed the steep red sandstone cliffs of Cape Parry and entered Whale Sound. Peary, unable to bear any weight on his leg, was strapped to a board like a piece of cargo. He was rowed ashore along with the expedition's supplies, including lumber to build a house and six tons of coal.

Before the *Kite* departed on July 30, with plans to pick up the expedition members twelve months later, Peary wrote several letters home. Among them was one to his mother, in which he praised Dr. Cook, calling him "patient, careful, and unruffled."

A two-room house was built according to a design drawn by Peary on the northeast shore of McCormick Bay. The smallest room, seven by twelve feet, was for himself and Jo; the larger room, twelve by fourteen feet, was shared by the other five expedition members. The walls were covered inside and out with tarpaper; wool blankets were hung on the inner walls as insulation; bunks were built. A single stove heated both rooms. It was christened Red Cliff House, for the red sandstone cliffs behind it.

At first, Jo Peary cooked for the men, but she soon turned the job over to Matt Henson. However, she supervised the preparation of a special feast in honor of Henson's twenty-fifth birthday on August 8, 1891. Three days later, another occasion was celebrated—the third wedding anniversary of Lieutenant Peary and his wife.

Peary exercised his leg daily, but it often swelled to three times its normal size, making walking impossible. In the autumn, Peary sent

Red sandstone cliffs were the backdrop for Peary's first base camp in Greenland. After the explorers built a house on the northeast edge of McCormick Bay, they named it Red Cliff House.

Red Cliff House, about twelve feet by twenty-one feet, was divided into two rooms and heated by a single stove.

Gibson, Astrup, Verhoeff and Cook inland to establish supply depots on the ice; his leg still hadn't healed well enough for him to go along.

As winter darkness settled over the Arctic, confinement of the expedition members inside Red Cliff House made Peary think he'd chosen some of them unwisely. He was disappointed in particular with John Verhoeff. The young man didn't get along with Jo Peary, insulted Matt Henson, and was rude to an Inuit couple, Manee and Ikwa, who'd befriended the expedition. Nor was Peary pleased with tall, strapping Langdon Gibson, who had an athlete's appetite but tended to be lazy.

Jo Peary had grievances of her own: she heartily disapproved of the Eskimo custom of exchanging wives.

Winter deepened. The men bickered among themselves and resented the awkwardness of having a woman in their midst. Peary himself became irritable. In his journal, Gibson called the lieutenant "the Invalid," and Verhoeff "the Crank." Nevertheless, some days were made interesting by visits from Eskimo families, and in December, Jo Peary prepared a Christmas celebration, followed by homemade chocolate ice cream on New Year's Eve.

By February 1892, Peary's leg had improved enough that he, Astrup, and Dr. Cook undertook a short journey across the inland ice. It almost was their last. The first night they took cover in a snow house the men had built earlier in the year. A sudden storm came up, collapsing the roof and burying the three men. Peary and Cook freed themselves, but Astrup became trapped. Peary opened a breathing hole for the young Norwegian and was able to pull him out of what had nearly become a tomb of snow and ice.

Another foray onto the ice cap began on May 3. This time, Peary took four men—Astrup, Cook, Gibson, and Henson. He'd obtained twenty Eskimo dogs to pull the sledges, which were lightly loaded with only enough food to last the trip, a Winchester rifle, ammunition, medical supplies, and navigation equipment. The dogs would also serve a grislier function: in case of a shortage of meat, some could be killed and fed to the other dogs—or to the men, if necessary.

Henson injured his heel and was the first to return to camp. After traveling 130 miles (210 kilometers) north across the ice cap, Cook and Gibson turned back, too. Peary and Astrup forged on with thirteen dogs. When the exhausted dogs refused to pull the sledges in the heavy snow, Peary and Astrup climbed into the traces to urge them on. Four of the animals died of *piblockto*, an Inuit name for a type of delirium caused when a driver insisted that dogs work harder than they reasonably

Peary didn't want to repeat the mistakes of earlier explorers. Instead of "manhauling" his way to the North Pole, he decided to use sledge dogs, as the Eskimos did.

could. Such animals refused food, attacked their teammates, and behaved as if they were rabid.

Astrup was stricken by what earlier explorers called "arctic fever," a state not unlike what the dogs suffered. Peary noted gloomily in his diary, "Feel less like writing than for last three or four days . . . have not yet been to the 82nd meridian. But I will do all that man may do."

After finding the tracks of musk oxen and hunting them down, the two men and the remaining dogs feasted on fresh meat. They reached the northeastern edge of Greenland's ice cap on July 4, 1892, more than three thousand feet (nine hundred meters) above a frozen bay that Peary named Independence Bay.

Their struggle over the inland ice had lasted six weeks and covered five hundred miles (eight hundred kilometers). Peary wanted to push on but knew he was still hundreds of miles from the Pole and had barely enough food left for the return trip to Red Cliff House. Only six dogs remained out of thirteen. Peary knew he must turn back, but was consoled by the belief that he'd proved that Greenland was an island, not part of a larger continent as had been supposed.

Musk oxen, covered with thick, shaggy coats, could tolerate severe arctic temperatures. They provided the explorers with fresh meat.

When the *Kite* returned to pick up the members of the expedition, not everyone made the journey home.

John Verhoeff, who was so obstinate about following orders that Dr. Cook labeled him "an insurgent type," had vanished while doing some final nature studies. Peary and the other team members carefully searched the area where Verhoeff had disappeared. They found tracks in the snow, but never again saw the young man himself.

The search team left a letter and cache of food behind and offered a reward to the Inuit people for information about Verhoeff's fate. Dr. Cook speculated that while trying to cross the ice at a point known for its bottomless crevasses, Verhoeff had fallen into one of them.

FINDING TRUE NORTH

Because the needle on a compass points to the magnetic pole, not to true north, Peary and the other polar explorers of his day often depended on a curious device called an artificial horizon, used whenever the sun could be clearly seen. A small, square wooden pan was filled with mercury. As the arctic sun approached its zenith (also called local apparent noon), two images of the sun appeared on the level, mirrorlike surface of the mercury. At the instant the edges of the two suns touched, a shadow cast by a man or by a pole stuck in the snow pointed to true north.

The supplies in Red Cliff House—pots, pans, knives, saws, scissors—were divided among the Inuits. The house itself was put in the care of Manee and Ikwa, with the promise that if the expedition didn't return the following year it would be theirs to keep.

The *Kite* left on its homeward voyage on August 24, 1892. Peary worried that Verhoeff's absence might reflect poorly on his reputation as a leader, because he was already planning to return to Whale Sound. He hadn't gotten to the Pole this time, but he was convinced that another expedition would put the white grail in his hands.

As Dr. Cook observed, once a man had "tasted the other world effects of the ice world, the lure becomes a permanent drawing power for life." So it did—for Peary, and for Cook himself.

The Inuits, whose name means "the real people," were called skraelings, "the wretched ones," by Eric the Red. They befriended Peary, providing him with guides and dogs.

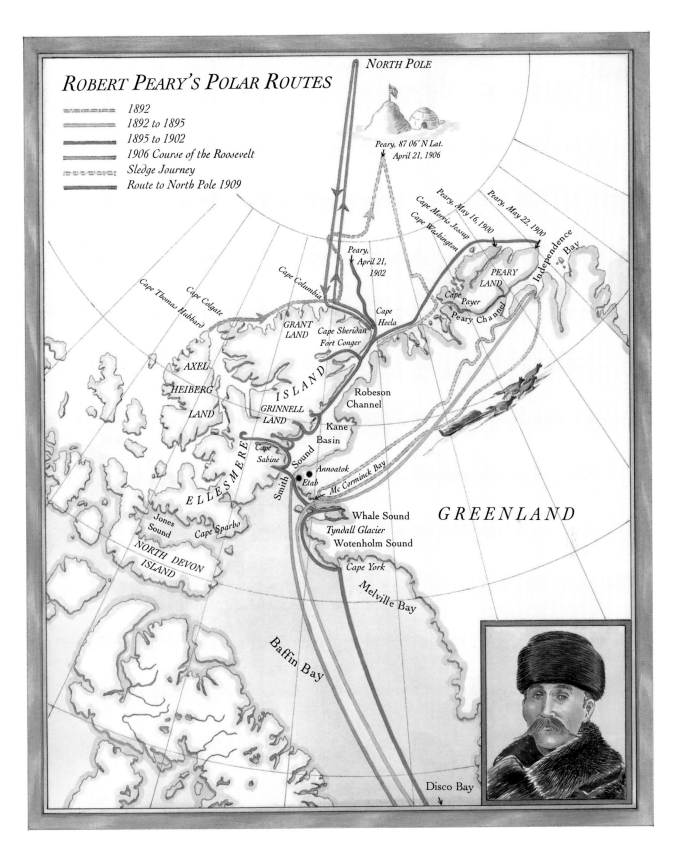

Robert Peary's Polar Routes

1892
1892 to 1895
1895 to 1902
1906 Course of the Roosevelt
Sledge Journey
Route to North Pole 1909

NORTH POLE

Peary, 87 06' N Lat.
April 21, 1906

Peary, May 16, 1900
Cape Morris Jessup
Cape Washington

Peary, May 22, 1900

Independence
Bay

Peary,
April 21,
1902

PEARY
LAND

Cape Payer

Cape Columbia

Peary Channel

Cape Sheridan
Fort Conger

Cape Hecla

GRANT
LAND

Cape Thomas Hubbard

Cape Colgate

AXEL

HEIBERG

LAND

ISLAND

GRINNELL
LAND

Robeson
Channel

Kane
Basin

Cape
Sabine

Smith
Sound

Annoatok

Etab

Mc Corminck Bay

ELLESMERE

GREENLAND

Jones
Sound

Cape Sparbo

NORTH DEVON
ISLAND

Whale Sound

Tyndall Glacier

Wotenholm Sound

Cape York

Melville Bay

Baffin Bay

Disco Bay

F I V E

Ahnighito, the Snow Baby

N

United States Navy claims highest discoveries on Greenland east coast, Independence Bay, 82° north latitude, 34° west longitude, discovered July 4, 1892. Greenland ice cap ends south of Victoria inlet.
—The New York Times, *September 13, 1892*

Peary believed he stood on the edge of the fame he'd told his mother he *must* have. Nevertheless, he downplayed his news in a telegram that he sent home from Newfoundland. But when the Kite docked in Philadelphia ten days later, the expedition was greeted with enthusiastic cheers.

Mattie Verhoeff, however, tearfully accused Peary of behaving badly toward her missing brother and reminded the lieutenant that Verhoeff had made a generous financial contribution to the expedition. It was a charge Peary had dreaded. There was little for him to say

Peary realized it would be wise to dress as the Inuits did—in layers of animal skins. One advantage of such clothing was that the material "breathed" and didn't soak up moisture.

except that he regretted the young man was not among those who had returned. No one knows what Peary thought about the warm letter he received congratulating him on "wonderful achievements and grand results" in the Arctic. It came from Fridtjof Nansen, whose account of his own trip across Greenland Peary had dismissed as "pretentious."

Peary asked the navy for a longer leave to pursue another assault on the Pole. Other officers—Annapolis graduates, members of the regular navy—were envious of the attention he attracted. They believed Peary was neglecting his naval duties to further his own ambitions, and they blocked his request. He was assigned instead to the Norfolk navy yard.

Doubts about Peary's claims of traveling so far north trickled in from France, Germany, and Norway, nations that had their own agendas for Arctic exploration. The president of the American Geographical Society supported Peary, however, and intervened on his behalf with the secretary of the navy for another leave for a second Greenland expedition.

As soon as the new leave was granted, Peary began to raise money for the trip, planned for 1893. He decided the fastest way to do that was to hire a booking agent, who could quickly arrange as many speeches as possible for the highest fees.

Peary tackled public appearances as energetically as he'd tackled exploration, giving 165 speeches in 103 days. He and Matt Henson appeared on stage dressed in their Arctic furs, along with five sledge dogs. Surrounded by other paraphernalia of the expedition—ice axes, harpoons, snowshoes, and a sledge—they earned nearly $20,000.

Choosing teammates for the Second Greenland Expedition was easier than it had been for the first trip because Peary believed he knew the type of men he was looking for. Henson, Astrup, and Cook were selected automatically. Dr. Cook, however, who had arctic dreams of his own, dropped out when Peary forbade him to write or speak about the first expedition or any others he went on.

Peary intended to write and lecture himself, and he didn't want his fame usurped by others. Therefore, all team members were required to sign a contract agreeing not to discuss their own Arctic experiences. Peary's determination to claim the public stage for himself under-

On his second trip to the Arctic, in 1893, Peary and his crew boarded the _Falcon_. Before the ship departed, sightseers were allowed on board for twenty-five cents each.

standably caused resentment among his teammates.

In Cook's place, Dr. Edwin Vincent was selected as the surgeon for the new expedition. To the amazement of family and friends, Jo Peary, four months pregnant, planned to return to Greenland too, accompanied by a nurse, Mrs. Susan J. Cross. Peary apparently forgot his own rule—that small parties were *always* more efficient—because this one, counting Henson and himself, numbered fourteen.

The Second Greenland Expedition (it was the third, if Peary's earliest trip with Maigaard is counted) left the United States on July 8, 1893, aboard the trim, black-hulled, yellow-masted *Falcon*. In a final fundraising effort, for twenty-five cents each, sightseers were allowed on board in Philadelphia, Brooklyn, Boston, and Portland as the ship headed up the coast.

After additional stops in Newfoundland, Labrador, and Greenland, the *Falcon* arrived at Inglefield Gulf on Greenland's western edge. There the expedition built a new base camp, which it finished in August 1893 and named Anniversary Lodge. Shortly after Peary's departure the year before, Red Cliff House had been destroyed by the Inuits, who had a superstitious dread of ghosts and feared Verhoeff's spirit would return to haunt them.

Then, on September 12, 1893, the fifteenth member of the expedition arrived, weighing eight pounds, eleven ounces. The Inuits marveled at the pale skin of the Pearys' infant daughter, Marie, and called her *Ahnighito*, or "the Snow Baby." Peary was so nervous around his infant daughter that he didn't trust himself to hold her until she was eighteen days old.

Peary hoped to accomplish more than he had on his previous expedition—to get all the way to the Pole this time—but he fared much worse. Historians have concluded that, because of the relative ease of his earlier accomplishments, he had planned the journey poorly. For example, although he intended to rely on dogs for transportation, he brought along eight burros, assuming they would be good pack animals for heavier loads. He also took pigeons to Greenland to relay messages from the explorers back to the base camp. The burros ended up as dog food. The pigeons froze to death.

Then, on Halloween 1893, while Peary was exploring five miles

Jo Peary accompanied her husband on his second voyage and gave birth to baby Marie (sixteen months old in this picture) on September 12, 1893. The Inuits called her Ahnighito, or "the Snow Baby."

from camp, part of an iceberg broke off Bowdoin Glacier (named in honor of his old college) in the bay in front of Anniversary Lodge. Huge waves crashed up on the beach, smashing a steam-powered launch. Worse, precious barrels of heating oil were washed out to sea. When informed of what had happened, Peary cried, "The fates and all hell are against me, but I'll conquer yet."

On March 6, 1894, Perry headed north with a party of seven team members, five Eskimos, and twelve sledges. Once again, the dogs were stricken by *piblockto*; in other words, they were worked to death. Astrup and Lee became ill, and Peary returned with them to the base camp. Peary headed north again, but the temperature dropped to -60 degrees Fahrenheit (-51 degrees Celsius), accompanied by winds of 48 miles per hour (77 kilometers per hour). Dogs froze to death where they slept. One team member's nose was badly frostbitten; snowblindness plagued Peary and others. Peary declared it was a storm that "beats the record as the most severe ever experienced by any Arctic Party."

On April 10, having gone a mere 128 miles (205 kilometers) from Anniversary Lodge, Peary realized he was still several hundred miles from Independence Bay, the northernmost point of his previous expedition. He turned back, discouraged to have accomplished so little.

Then he recalled stories he'd heard about an "iron mountain" near Cape York and the knives made by Inuits from the iron.

The metal probably came from meteorites, Peary correctly assumed. If he could retrieve a sample of the material, at least he wouldn't have to return to the United States empty-handed. However, the Inuits had never revealed the location of the iron deposits to outsiders.

Peary offered a young hunter a rifle to take him to where the *saviksue*, or "great irons," were located, and set out in May 1894 to find them. Snowstorms, broken ice, and open water would have dissuaded a less determined man, but Peary found one meteorite the Eskimos called "the woman," weighing about 5,500 pounds (2,500 kilograms), and another, "the dog," about 1,000 pounds (450 kilograms). Peary scratched the initial *P* on the largest meteorite to document his discovery, but the transportation of such heavy objects was left until later.

When the *Falcon* returned to Greenland in late summer, Peary—still smarting with disappointment over the outcome of the second expedition—decided to remain in the Arctic for another year.

When he asked the other team members who would stay behind for a fourth expedition, planned for the spring of 1895, only Matt Hensen and young Hugh Lee volunteered. The others, Astrup among them, resented what they considered Peary's imperious behavior and refused to continue. In Peary's opinion, such men were simply cowards.

For safety's sake, however, Mrs. Peary and the Snow Baby went home on August 26, 1894. Peary watched as the white handkerchief his wife waved from her cabin window disappeared in the distance, and wondered if his daughter would recognize him when she saw him next.

"Will she always be as bright and quick and strong and healthy as she is now . . . what will be her fate in life, happy or unhappy?" he asked himself. It was the first of many times Peary's powerful obsession with the Pole would lure him away from the family he loved.

S I X

I Shall Find a Way or Make One

I lay helpless on my back for six weeks. . . . Still I never lost faith.
—Robert Peary, 1899, at Fort Conger, on Ellesmere Island

In April 1895, Peary reached out again to seize the white grail, accompanied by loyal Henson and Lee, plus six Eskimos and more than sixty sledge dogs. Trouble began immediately. Food and other supplies that had been cached earlier in the year were impossible to find. Harsh weather forced the Inuits to turn back, taking some of the dogs with them. In a mishap, Hugh Lee's sledge was smashed beyond repair. Several of the remaining dogs died or were killed for food.

Five hundred miles inland, with eleven dogs left and supplies running out, Peary and Henson hunted for fresh meat. They returned with a single rabbit. A day later, musk oxen were sighted, and five were

On June 25, 1895, when Peary and other expedition members returned to base after a fourth attempt to reach the North Pole, the only sledge dog left alive was the brave Panikpah.

killed. They were skinned on the spot, their bloody flesh eaten raw, so warm with recent life it steamed in the freezing air.

On the return trip to Anniversary Lodge, young Lee became so ill that he begged to be left to die. "We will all get home or none of us will," Peary replied. He made camp and nursed Lee with a diet of meat broth and brandy until he was well enough to go on. "He was gentle and kind," Lee remembered, "which is true greatness."

When the expedition got back to base camp on June 25, 1895, having failed to reach the Pole, only one dog—Panikpah—was left alive. Before he ate his own dinner, Peary fed the starving animal by hand. For a week after their return, all three men suffered the mental confusion that can attack those who spend too much time on the polar ice under brutal conditions. For example, Peary overheard his companions talking among themselves and believed they were plotting against him. He suspected that Henson, who'd always been faithful to a fault, might try to poison him. "I wonder if I am really going mad," he confessed in his diary.

Nevertheless, something important had been learned on a journey that otherwise seemed a failure. Peary had always hoped he'd find a smooth, icy highway from Independence Bay straight north to the Pole. He knew at last that no such highway existed. If he intended to seize the elusive grail, he'd have to find another route.

Peary dreaded seeing the relief ship, the *Kite*, arrive to pick him up. But there was one last thing he could do to add luster to his two years in the Arctic: He ordered the ship to return to Cape York, where the iron meteorites were loaded on board.

When he was on the ship—warm and heading home, with decent food and a chance to rest—Peary's spirits lifted enough that he began to think about the next expedition. Hugh Lee wrote, "Peary was a very determined man; he was absolutely ruthless, so far as punishing his own flesh was concerned." Peary's admirers and detractors agreed: He never asked a man to endure more than he was willing to endure himself.

Fortunately for Peary's future ambitions, the rest of the world was easier on him than he was on himself. He was awarded a gold medal by the American Geographical Society in 1897, and it was followed by one from the Royal Geographical Society of London in 1898. The publicity helped him raise money for another trip, and the meteorites were sold to the American Museum of Natural History for $40,000. Peary was criticized, however, for looting artifacts that many believed belonged to the Inuits.

Peary knew he must have two things besides money: another leave from the navy, and a ship powerful enough to carry him farther north than any of his earlier vessels. He intended to force his way up through Smith Sound and the Kane Basin to the very edge of the frozen Arctic Ocean.

But instead of granting him the five-year leave he requested, navy officials (who still wanted to get him out of the public eye) ordered him to report to Mare Island, on the west coast of the United States. His superiors chafed at his constant requests for leave, partly because Peary

Before Peary returned to New York after his fourth failed assault on the North Pole, he returned to Cape York, where he loaded some <u>saviksue</u>, or iron meteorites, on board ship. The Eskimos used such iron to make knives.

continued to be paid half his regular salary while away.

A few days before he was set to depart for California, a close friend of President William McKinley prevailed on the newly elected president to grant Peary permission to continue his quest. Morris K. Jesup, the wealthy, influential president of the American Geographical Society and founder of the YMCA, urged fourteen of his friends to underwrite a new expedition, guaranteeing Peary four thousand dollars a year for the next four years. Later, Jesup organized the contributors into the Peary Arctic Club. A British admirer, Alfred Harmsworth, publisher of the *Daily Mail*, offered Peary a steam-powered yacht, the *Windward*.

Such support was more welcome than ever. Peary had learned that a Norwegian explorer, Otto Sverdrup—one of the skiers who'd accompanied Nansen on the first crossing of the Greenland ice cap in

Morris K. Jesup gave Robert Peary important financial assistance.

1888—was headed for exactly the same area along the coast of Ellesmere Island where he intended to launch his next assault on the Pole. Those pesky Norwegians!

Peary had already named the path he intended to take "the American route" and accused Sverdrup of an "unprincipled attempt" to capitalize on Peary's own efforts to get to the Pole. He got back to the Arctic in late summer for what would become a four-year expedition (1898-1902). In October 1898, Peary unexpectedly came upon Sverdrup's camp. The Norwegian explorer—who had as much right to be there as Peary—invited his American competitor to join him for a cup of coffee. Peary haughtily refused. It was a display of poor sportsmanship that Sverdrup never forgot.

Peary was so afraid the Norwegian might make a base camp at Fort Conger, the site he'd chosen for himself on the upper northeast edge of Ellesmere Island, that he decided in late December to make a dash for it. Within a few days of beginning the hasty journey, Peary fell on the ice, temporarily paralyzing his right arm. The temperature dropped to –50 degrees Fahrenheit (–46 degrees Celsius). When two of his Inuit companions become too numbed by cold to travel on, Peary urged them to bury themselves in the snow, along with nine of the weaker dogs, to keep them all from freezing until they could make their way back to the ship.

Peary and the others hurried on, and on January 6 they stumbled upon a camp that had been abandoned fifteen years earlier by the U.S. Signal Corps. Peary, Henson, and Dr. Dedrick, the surgeon for the expedition, forced open the entrance of the dwelling, lighted their oil stove, and made tea to warm themselves. Only then did Peary notice what he described as a "suspicious wooden feeling" in both feet.

Henson and Dedrick cut away Peary's *kamiks*, or Eskimo boots. His legs were white to the knees, his toes so badly frozen that two of them snapped off like twigs from a dead tree. Dedrick removed parts of seven other toes that were too damaged to be saved. Additional surgery later left Peary with only the nub of a little toe on each foot.

For six weeks Peary lay helpless. In a letter to Jo he dismissed the mishap as "of no importance," but he knew that the Arctic was no place for a man with such a disability. The outlook for the future was bleaker than it had ever been. Yet on the wall beside his bunk at Fort Conger, Peary scrawled a quotation from the Roman philosopher Seneca: *Inveniam viam aut faciam*, "I shall find a way or make one."

Reports of Peary's misfortune persuaded the Peary Arctic Club to ask Dr. Frederick Cook to assist in a search for his former leader. Cook's assignment was to assess Peary's ability to continue his quest for the Pole. Cook reported that he found "an iron man, wrecked in ambition, wrecked in physique, wrecked in hope"—but a man who nevertheless refused to abandon his dream.

In April 1901, Peary, Henson, and one of the Inuits again headed north from Ellesmere Island, but after several days they were forced back. In 1902 another assault on the Pole—the sixth—was made, again from the northernmost tip of Ellesmere Island. Rough ice forced the men to zigzag back over their own tracks, to man-haul the sledges over ice barriers, and to hack out a path with axes. It was killing work, and they were forced back again, but not before they had reached 84° N., a new farthest north record for the United States.

By this time, Peary was an Arctic veteran, having spent sixteen years in constant pursuit of the white grail, longer than any explorer from any nation. On his birthday in May 1902, Peary reflected that he was forty-six years old, "too old for this kind of work."

In spite of his efforts, the Pole remained as mysterious as ever. Peary asked himself in his diary, "Has the game been worth the candle?" In youth he'd taken hold of a dream to reach the Pole; now, in middle age, it had taken hold of him. For better or worse, Robert Edwin Peary had no choice but to continue his search.

CONFLICT AND CONTRADICTION

The life of Peary the explorer was filled with conflict and contradiction. Not surprisingly, so was the life of Peary the man.

While recovering from the damage to his feet, Peary received news that brave Jo had borne him a second daughter, Francine. He never saw the child, for she died in August 1899 at age seven months. "I shall never be quite the same again," Jo Peary told her husband.

Peary also learned that his mother, who had devoted her life to her only child, had died. She had welcomed death, a cousin wrote, because she believed her beloved Bertie, whom she hadn't seen in four years, had already died in a far-off land.

His grieving wife learned that Peary had also become the father of a part-Inuit son. The boy, Anaukak, whom he never acknowledged for fear of public scandal, was borne of his relationship with a young Inuit woman, Allakasingwah, nicknamed Ally. In 1906, Ally bore Peary a second son, Kali. Many years later, one of Peary's Inuit grandsons, Peter, made it to the North Pole himself—not once, but twice.

SEVEN

The Thing That I Must Do

I began to long for . . . the silence and the vastness of the great, white lonely North.

—Robert Peary, describing how he felt between expeditions, 1907

Public and political admiration for Peary's courage resulted in his promotion to the rank of navy commander. Again he attracted the support of a powerful backer—President Theodore Roosevelt—a lover of adventure himself, who understood Peary's need to pursue his quest. Even the birth in 1903 of a son, Robert Jr., couldn't keep the elder Peary from a seventh expedition to the Arctic.

By March 1905, with the help of the Peary Arctic Club, Peary had built a new, more powerful ship, designed according to his own specifications. He named it the *Roosevelt*, but often called it the *Teddy*. The sturdy egg-shaped vessel, powered by both steam and sail, was

Peary designed a special ship, powered by both steam and sail, that he hoped would break through the Arctic ice more easily than other vessels he had used. He named it the Roosevelt, in honor of President Theodore Roosevelt.

only 184 feet long, enabling it to turn quickly through ice-choked Arctic waters.

When the *Roosevelt* sailed from New York in July 1905, Matt Henson was at Peary's side as he'd been on all other expeditions. Henson had become a special favorite of the Inuits. He was a man of color, but more than that, he was admired for his skill as a sledge driver and his generosity in sharing the proceeds of a hunt.

Bad luck plagued Peary as it had on every other journey. The *Roosevelt*, even with its three-foot-thick sides and interior steel bracing, was damaged by the ice. Several of its coal-fired steam boilers were defective, forcing the ship to travel at half power.

Treacherous "leads" prevented steady travel by sledge over the ice.

Matthew Henson was a favorite of the Eskimos. He wrote about his Arctic adventures in *A Black Explorer at the North Pole*.

Life on board the <u>Roosevelt</u> was crowded after Eskimo families were taken aboard in Greenland. They brought with them sledge dogs that would be used when the expedition headed north across the polar ice.

(A lead is a stretch of open water that begins as a crack in the ice no wider than a thin black ribbon, but can expand to several hundred feet across because of the shift of the ocean below.) In addition, Peary underestimated how far the drift of sea ice would carry him from his goal.

Before giving up his latest effort to get to the Pole, however, Peary achieved a new farthest north record for the United States, 87° N. Discouraged, he turned for home, arriving in New York on Christmas Eve 1905. Having been defeated so often, observers wondered if the weatherbeaten navy commander, whose sliding gait was a reminder of how badly his feet were damaged in 1899, had the courage to try again.

Yes, Peary told an audience of the National Geographic Society: "To me the final and complete solution of the polar mystery . . . is the thing which must be done for the honor and credit of this country, the thing which it is intended that I should do, and the thing that I must do."

As Peary waited for the *Roosevelt* to be repaired for an eighth expedition, he wasn't concerned by rumors that Dr. Frederick Cook also was planning a trip to the Arctic. "Cook is an honorable man," he assured friends after he was told that Cook intended to help a wealthy sportsman, John R. Bradley, hunt for polar bear.

A greater problem was posed by the death of Peary's influential supporter, Morris Jesup. For years, Jesup had provided needed financial

Open water, or a "lead," could halt an expedition in its tracks. Men and dogs had to wait for "young ice" to form before they could travel on.

assistance. Peary was relieved when Jesup's widow made a donation to the next expedition in her husband's memory.

For the first time, Peary didn't have to beg or pull strings to get a leave from the navy. His superiors now agreed with the rest of America that national pride was involved in the undertaking.

President Roosevelt came aboard before Peary sailed from New York in July 1908. "I believe in you, Peary," he boomed in his hearty way. The encouragement may have made Peary feel worse, not better. He was keenly aware that he was fifty-two years old. He knew that time was running out.

No sooner had Peary arrived in the Arctic than he came across the path of Dr. Cook, though not the man himself—Cook had already headed north and hadn't been heard from in months. Peary became alarmed. Observers reported that he'd taken off across the ice not with Mr. Bradley but with two native companions, twenty-six dogs, and few supplies. *What, exactly, was Cook up to?*

Peary established a new base camp at Cape Columbia, on the northernmost tip of Ellesmere Island. Straight ahead, 475 miles (766 kilometers) as the arrow flies, lay the white grail. This time Peary plotted his route slightly west of due north, to allow for the eastward drift of the polar ice that had sabotaged his previous trip.

Expedition members were divided into four teams that worked in relays to break a trail and keep it open. Peary planned to follow with dogs that were well rested and well fed, then make a final dash for the Pole.

Peary realized what was at stake. "I knew it was my last game upon the great Arctic chessboard," he admitted in his book *The North Pole.* "It was win this time or be forever defeated."

After twenty-three years, Peary had learned to expect the unexpected in the frozen north. He wasn't disappointed this time. In October, 80 of the 246 sledge dogs he'd taken on board at Etah, Greenland, died from eating rotten whale meat. On the morning of his departure on February 28, 1909, no open water could be seen to the north, but a month later the expedition ran into what Peary called the Big Lead. If a lead was narrow enough, a crossing could be made with a bridge of sledges, but this time it was necessary to wait several days for "young" ice to become thick enough to support men, supplies, and dogs.

Pressure ridges as tall as buildings, caused by ice floes colliding with each other, further stalled progress. A wind out of the east, called Tornarsuk ("the devil") by the Inuits, was fierce, and temperatures dropped to –50 degrees Fahrenheit (–46 degrees Celsius). The Arctic seemed more determined than ever to keep its secrets to itself.

By March, the main team composed of Peary, Henson, Captain Bob Bartlett, and their Inuit guides reached 87° N.; the Pole was still nearly 150 miles (240 kilometers) away. Peary picked the men who would accompany him on the final dash: only Henson and four Inuits—Egingwah, Seeglo, Ootah, and Ooqueah. Bartlett, the captain of the *Roosevelt*, who'd been with Peary on other expeditions, had hoped to share the joy of reaching the Pole and wept when he was sent back to base camp.

On April 5, 1909, Peary exclaimed in his diary, "Over the 89th!" The next day he estimated that he was at least within three nautical miles of the Pole. A snowhouse was built, and as Henson and the Inuits watched, Peary set an American flag atop the shelter. He named it Camp Morris K. Jesup in honor of his longtime benefactor. The flag had special meaning: Jo Peary had made it for him many years before.

Peary took several chronometer and sextant readings, confirming that he'd passed 89° N. Then he left Henson and the Inuits behind as he journeyed—*alone*—across the final few miles. The next day, additional readings convinced him he was at the magical point where north, south, east, and west became one.

"The Pole at last!!!" he wrote in his diary. "The prize of three centuries. My dream and goal for twenty-three years. *Mine*, at last." (The italics are Peary's.) His life's work had been completed. "The thing that was intended from the beginning that I should do . . . I have done."

A tragedy marred the victory. When Peary boarded the *Roosevelt* for the trip home, he heard that Ross Marvin of Cornell University, one of his favorite expedition members, had fallen through the ice while on his way back to base camp earlier and had drowned. Many years later, the truth came out: Marvin had been shot in a dispute with some of

---

After trying for twenty-three years to reach the North Pole, Robert Peary finally did, on April 6, 1909. "<u>Mine</u>, at last," he wrote in his diary.

the Inuits, and his body had been dumped through a hole in the ice. But more devastating news lay in store for Robert E. Peary. Before he could reach Newfoundland to send an official telegram announcing the greatest achievement of his life, Frederick A. Cook suddenly emerged from the Arctic wildneress. The doctor was welcomed by cheering crowds in Copenhagen after astonishing the world with an announcement of his own: He had reached the Pole—on April 21, 1908—*one full year* earlier than Peary.

Before Peary had a chance to savor the sweetness of victory, the white grail was snatched from his grasp.

Frederick Cook, Peary's greatest rival, pictured in the Arctic with his expedition.

EIGHT

Fame Too Dearly Bought?

I pulled the thing off finally, and then have the whole matter soiled and smirched by a cowardly cur.
  —Robert E. Peary, 1910, contesting Dr. Frederick Cook's claims

Peary called Cook a liar and dismissed his announcement, which in turn caused critics to denounce *him* as a poor loser. Often haughty and tactless, Peary had made his share of enemies, many of whom stepped forward now, Otto Sverdrup and Thomas Dedrick among them.

When the *Roosevelt* steamed into New York, Peary's dream of cheering crowds and marching bands turned into a nightmare: There were only jeers from Cook's supporters. By contrast, the doctor, who'd arrived in New York first, had been welcomed by 100,000 fans and handed the keys to the city.

In Pittsburgh, a newspaper poll showed that 73,238 readers

believed Cook's claims; only 2,814 took Peary's side. In Ohio, a similar poll favored Cook 55 to 1. Stunned, Peary retreated to the home he'd built on Eagle Island, off the Maine coast.

After Cook submitted his proof of having reached the Pole to Danish experts in Copenhagen, however, they ruled in December 1909 that it failed to support his claim. The Inuits who'd accompanied Cook admitted that they'd never been out of sight of land. Others noted that Cook's sledge showed no signs of the hard wear one would expect after a journey of more than a thousand miles.

On the other hand, critics were equally skeptical about Peary's evidence, which he withheld for months because he feared that Cook would use it to promote his own claims. There was an aura of mystery surrounding Peary's final trip to the Arctic; it persists to this day, and remains the basis of lively argument among modern polar historians:

Why was Robert Bartlett, the only man with the navigational expertise that would be respected by critics, sent back to base camp five days before Peary made a final dash for the Pole?

Why did Peary go alone those last few miles to the top of the world, taking with him no one who could verify his mathematical calculations?

Why was Peary's declaration, "The Pole at last!!!" written on a separate piece of paper and inserted into his diary, as if it were added later?

Why were several pages in Peary's North Pole diary blank?

Why was the handwriting in Peary's North Pole diary so regular and even—not a cramped, hasty scrawl as would be expected from a man writing under stressful conditions?

Why were the geographical calculations Peary jotted down so vague and inconclusive?

Why had Peary placed his hands over his eyes and refused a congratulatory handshake from Matt Henson on the day he had supposedly achieved his life's goal?

Why was Peary so preoccupied on the return trip to base camp—not as if he were a victor, but like a man who carried a great weight on his shoulders?

Even the National Geographic Society was at first wary of Peary's claims. Only after studying them did a panel of three judges decide that Peary had reached the North Pole. Mathematicians at the U.S. Coast and Geodetic Survey in Washington, D.C., concluded he had come "within a stone's throw" of the Pole.

In March 1910, the U.S. Congress investigated the matter, which Peary found especially humiliating. It was as if he were on trial, being cross-examined by men he considered to be his inferiors. Finally, in March 1911, a congressional bill was passed approving Peary's retirement from the navy with a full pension and the rank of admiral, backdated to April 6, 1909, the date he claimed to have reached the Pole.

Europeans were kinder to Peary—he was awarded twenty-two gold medals, plus the French Legion of Honor. Among three honorary doctorates was one bestowed on him by the University of Edinburgh. Nevertheless, the Cook controversy tarnished the bright gleam of the white grail that Peary had pursued for a lifetime.

Between 1909 and 1920, the admiral, Jo, and their two children divided their time between a home in Washington, D.C., and their summer place on Eagle Island. Peary continued as the president of the American Geographical Society, a post he'd been elected to in 1903. He wrote many books and articles, gave lectures at one thousand dollars per appearance, and became a wealthy man.

When the United States entered World War I in 1917, in spite of his age, Peary volunteered for duty. His offer couldn't be accepted because a physical examination revealed that he had pernicious anemia. Transfusions were started, which prolonged the admiral's life but could not cure the disease.

In 1919, Robert E. Peary spent a final summer on his beloved Eagle

Island, often resting in the sun on a rug made from the hide of an Arctic musk ox. He died in Washington, D.C., on February 20, 1920, a few months shy of his sixty-fourth birthday, and was buried in Arlington National Cemetery.

Jo Peary blamed the Cook affair for shortening her husband's life. "No one will ever know how the attack on my husband's veracity affected him. . . . [It] did more toward the breaking down of his iron constitution than anything experienced in his explorations."

Dr. Cook's fame was brief. He was discredited by most experts in the United States and Europe, and in 1923, he was sentenced to nearly

In spite of the scandal created by Frederick Cook's claim to have reached the North Pole before Peary, the admiral was welcomed like a hero in cities such as London.

fifteen years in a federal prison at Leavenworth, Kansas, for his role in an oil-lease scheme. He died in 1940, without retracting his claim about reaching the Pole, and wrote at the end of his life, "Some credit for original discovery should go on my grave."

The question still hangs over Peary's accomplishment: Did he get to the top of the world, as he claimed? With the use of modern measuring devices, most polar experts believe that Peary probably came within sixty to one hundred miles of the precise Pole.

Controversy centers not only around Peary's sextant readings and astronomical calculations, but also around the mileage he claimed— forty miles (65 kilometers) per day—during his final trip over the polar ice. By comparison, Fridtjof Nansen, respected for his experience as well as his integrity, averaged only twenty-five miles (40 kilometers) per day. Britain's Wally Herbert, who in 1968 made the longest Arctic dog-sledge trip ever recorded—3,720 miles (6,000 kilometers)—managed 26 miles (42 kilometers) per day under ideal conditions.

In 1982, two Norwegian explorers made a trip to the Pole by snowmobile that took fifty-seven days. In 1986, an American, Will Steger, reached the Pole by dog-sled in fifty-six days. Peary, by contrast, claimed to have made the same journey in thirty-seven days, which many experts consider unlikely.

Furthermore, Peary claimed to have made the 500-mile (800-kilometer) return trip to his base camp on Ellesmere Island in the unheard-of time of seventeen days!

How should readers interpret the puzzle of Robert Peary's amazing life? It might be well to remember that heroes are men before they are heroes. They are as fallible as ordinary mortals, compelled by longings of the human heart that can't be easily explained.

Peary himself had admitted, "I knew it was my last game upon the great Arctic chessboard. It was win this time or be forever defeated." Is it possible that the prospect of another failure was so painful that Peary told the world he'd reached a place at the top of the world when, in fact, he knew he hadn't? He took the answer to that question with him to the grave.

Admirers and critics agree, however, that Robert E. Peary struggled courageously for nearly a quarter century and endured greater hardship than any man of his day as he searched for the white grail. The young man from Portland, Maine, who longed to experience "the restless wild essence of life," had done exactly that.

A MYSTERY SOLVED

By the close of the twentieth century, the North Pole had been reached by snowmobile, airplane, balloon, submarine, and nuclear-powered ice breaker. The location of the Pole isn't a mystery anymore: It can be easily and accurately determined by the satellite-based Global Positioning Systems (GPS).

Arctic Timeline

320 b.c. Pytheas, Greek sailor from colony of Massilia, reports finding northern land where skies are light at midnight

A.D. 860 Ottar, Norse adventurer, sets first "farthest north" record by sailing around northern tip of Norway, reaches 72° N.

A.D. 984 Eric the Red, exiled from Norway for murder, settles on east coast of Greenland

1330 Rune stone near Upernavik, Greenland, proves Norsemen reached 73° N.

1350 Ivar Bardarsson, Norse settler in Greenland, reports open polar sea to the north

1372 Spanish and Portugese whalers make their way into Arctic

1527 Robert Thorne, English merchant, urges King Henry VIII to fund expedition to discover the Northwest Passage or Northeast Passage.

1569 Gerardus Mercator, mapmaker, charts polar region, assumes presence of open sea

1576 English adventurer Martin Frobisher begins first of three expeditions to Baffin Island

1587 John Davis, also English, gives his name to Davis Strait between west coast of Greenland and Nova Scotia

1596 Willem Barents discovers Spitzbergen archipelago, stopped by ice at 80° N.

1607 Henry Hudson, employed by Muscovy Company, reaches 80° N. as he searches for the Northeast Passage

Arctic Timeline

1611   After mutinous uprising, Hudson's crew sets him adrift

1616   William Baffin sets out from England aboard the *Discovery* to find elusive Northwest Passage; effort fails; exploration lags for one hundred years

1728   Vitus Bering, a Russian explorer, sails through strait between Russia and Alaska that bears his name

1765   Admiral Chichagov sent by empress of Russia to cross polar sea; stopped by ice at 80° N.

1773   Constantine Phipps, of British Royal Navy, stopped by ice at 80° N. as he attempts to go over Pole

1806   William Scoresby, English whaling captain, sails north along east coast of Greenland to 81° N., besting previous records

1818   England sends four-ship expedition into Arctic; included are men whose names become famous in polar history: Sir John Franklin, Edward Parry, John Ross, and James Clare Ross

1827   Edward Parry sets out on first "manhauling" expedition over arctic ice; his record of 82° N. stands for 48 years

1845   John Franklin leads the *Erebus* and *Terror* into Arctic; both vessels become trapped by ice; all aboard perish

1850   Dr. Elisha Kane joins arctic expedition funded by Henry Grinnell

1853   Kane returns to Arctic as leader of his own expedition

1856   Kane publishes *Arctic Explorations*, later read by both Robert E. Peary and Frederick A. Cook

1869   Germany sends two ships, the *Germania* and *Hansa*, to follow earlier route plotted by William Scoresby

1871 United States sends Charles Francis Hall to establish America's claim to polar regions; Hall dies, perhaps poisoned by his own men

1872 Austro-Hungarian expedition aboard the *Tegethoff* attempts to reach Pole via Novaya Zemlya, a stretch of islands jutting out from Russian mainland

1872 England sends Captain George Nares to reclaim farthest north record; a member of his party, Albert Hastings Markham, does, 83°N.

1881 Lieutenant Adolphus Greely, commanding the *Proteus*, names his camp on Ellesmere Island Fort Conger; establishes record of 83° for United States.

1883 A.E. Nordenskjold explores Greenland's ice cap for Sweden

1886 Robert E. Peary makes his first excursion onto Greenland ice cap in search of North Pole

1888 Fridtjof Nansen and five companions ski across Greenland ice cap at narrowest southern end

1891 Peary makes second trip to Greenland (called First Expedition); fails to reach Pole

1893 Peary organizes "Second Expedition" (his third trip to Greenland); fails again to reach Pole

1894-1905 Peary tries unsuccessfully for fourth, fifth, sixth, and seventh times to reach Pole

1908 Peary begins eighth—and final—trip to Arctic

1909 Peary announces he has reached the North Pole; Frederick A. Cook claims he already reached it one year earlier, in April 1908

1911 United States recognizes Peary's claim as legitimate discoverer of North Pole

Further Research

Books:

Dolan, Sean. *Matthew Henson: Arctic Explorer.* New York; Chelsea House Publishers, 1992.

Dwyer, Christopher. *Robert Peary and the Quest for the North Pole.* New York; Chelsea House Publishers, 1992.

Kent, Zachary. *The Story of Admiral Peary at the North Pole.* Chicago: Children's Press, 1988.

Websites:

Encyclopedia Britannica: Peary, Robert Edwin.
www.britannica.com (then search for Robert Edwin Peary)

Robert Edwin Peary: Historical Information.
www.arlingtoncemetery.org

Robinson, Verne: The 1909 Peary Arctic Club Expedition to the North Pole.
www.matthewhenson.com

Bibliography

Anderson, Madelyn Klein. *Robert E. Peary and the Fight for the Pole.* New York: Franklin Watts, 1992.

Borup, George. *A Tenderfoot with Peary.* New York: Frederick A. Stokes, 1911.

Bryce, Robert M. *Cook & Peary: The Polar Controversy, Resolved.* Mechanicsburg, PA: Stackpole, 1997.

Cook, Frederick A. *Return from the Pole.* New York: Pellegrini & Cudahy, 1951.

Bibliography

Dolan, Edward F., Jr, *Matthew Henson:* Black Explorer, New York: Dodd, Mead, 1979.

Fisher, David E. *Across the Top of the World: To the North Pole by Sled, Balloon, Airplane and Nuclear Icebreaker.* New York: Random House, 1992.

Freuchen, Peter. *Book of Arctic Exploration.* New York: Coward-McCann, 1962.

Green, Fitzhugh. *Peary: The Man Who Refused to Fail.* New York: G.P. Putnam's Sons, 1926.

Hall, Sam. *The Fourth World: The Heritage of the Arctic and Its Destruction.* New York: Alfred A. Knopf, 1987.

Henson, Matthew A. *A Black Explorer at the North Pole.* New York: Walker, 1969.

Herbert, Wally. *Across the Top of the World: The Last Great Journey on Earth.* New York: G.P. Putnam's Sons, 1971.

Herbert, Wally. *The Noose of Laurels: Robert E. Peary and the Race to the North Pole.* New York: Atheneum, 1989.

Holland, Clive (editor). *Farthest North: A History of North Polar Exploration in Eye-Witness Accounts.* New York: Carroll & Graf, 1994.

Hunt, William R. *To Stand at the Pole: The Dr. Cook-Admiral Peary North Pole Controversy.* New York: Stein & Day, 1981.

Kirwan, Laurence P. *A History of Polar Exploration.* New York: W.W. Norton, 1960.

Lopez, Barry H. *Artic Dreams. Imagination and Desire in a Northern Land-scape.* New York: Scribner's, 1986.

Lord, Walter. *Peary to the Pole.* New York: Harper & Row, 1963.

Lynch, Wayne. *A is for Arctic: Natural Wonders of a Polar World.* Buffalo, NY: Firefly Books, 1996.

MacMillan, Donald B. *Four Years in the White North.* Boston: Hale, Cushman, and Flint, 1933.

Malaurie, Jean. *The Last Kings of Thule: With the Polar Eskimos, as They Vace Their Destiny.* New York: Dutton, 1982.

Bibliography

Mirsky, Jeannette. *To the Arctic! The Story of Northern Exploration from Earliest Times to the Present.* New York: Alfred A. Knopf, 1948.

Mowat, Farley. *The Polar Passion: The Quest for the North-Pole, with Selections from Arctic Journals.* Boston: Little, Brown, 1967.

Owen, Russell. *The Conquest of the North and South Poles: Adventures of the Peary and Bryd Expeditions.* Eau Claire, WI: E.M. Hale, 1952.

Peary, Josephine Diebitsch. *My Artic Journal.* New York: Contemporary Publishing Co., 1893.

Peary, Robert E. *Northward Over the "Great Ice."* New York: Frederick A. Stokes, 1898.

Peary, Robert E. *Nearest the Pole: A Narrative of the Polar Expedition of the Peary Arctic Club in the S.S. Roosevelt, 1905-1906.* New York: Doubleday, Page, 1907.

Peary, Robert E. *The North Pole: Its Discovery in 1909 Under the Auspices of the Peary Arctic Club.* New York: Frederick A. Stokes, 1910.

Rawlins, Dennis. *Peary at the North Pole: Fact or Fiction.* Washington: Robert B. Luce, 1973.

Peary, Marie Ahnighito. *The Snowbaby's Own Story.* New York: Frederick A. Stokes, 1934.

Weems, John E. *Peary: The Explorer and the Man.* Boston: Houghton Mifflin, 1967.

Wright, Theon. *The Big Nail: The Story of the Cook-Peary Feud.* New York: John Day, 1970.

Source Notes

Chapter 1

8 "...wee saw the first Ice...": Clive Holland, editor, *Farthest North: A History of North Polar Exploration in Eye-Witness Accounts* (Carroll & Graf, 1994), p. 6.

8 "curdled": Laurence P. Kirwan, *A History of Polar Exploration* (W.W. Norton, 1960), p. 4.

Chapter 2

14 "I don't want to live and die...": Robert M. Bryce, *Cook & Peary: The Polar Controversy, Resolved* (Stackpole, 1997), p. 19.

16 "jingle": Wally Herbert, *The Noose of Laurels: Robert E. Peary and the Race to the North Pole* (Atheneum, 1989), p. 37.

17 "brilliant": Bryce, p. 16.

17 "he seemed...": John E. Weems, *Peary: The Explorer and the Man* (Houghton Mifflin, 1967), p. 23.

17 "every spot will have felt....": Bryce, p. 17.

19 "What have I done?...": Herbert, p. 45.

19 "Many men....": Weems, p. 47.

19 "Give me thy restless...": Weems, p. 34.

Chapter 3

20 "I never for a moment...": Bryce, p. 21.

21 "The time has arrived...": Weems, p. 69.

21 "impatient to reach...": Weems, p. 76.

22 "brought my name before the world": Weems, p. 84.

22 "I must have fame...": Bryce, p. 22.

22 "Such fame is dearly bought": Weems, p. 84.

25 "a pretentious affair": Weems, p. 99.

26 "absolutely essential to success": Weems, p. 104.

27 "the queerest, dirtiest-looking individuals": Josephine Diebitsch Peary, *My Arctic Journal* (Contemporary Publishing, 1894), p. 41.

27 "What the future will bring ...": Josephine Peary, p. 220.

Chapter 4

29 "It seems almost sure....": Weems, p. 124.

31 "patient, careful, and unruffled": Bryce, p. 37.

34 "the Invalid...the Crank": Bryce, p. 53.

35 "Feel less like writing....": Weems, p. 124.

37 "an insurgent type": Bryce, p. 73.

38 "tasted the other world...." Bryce, p. 83.

Chapter 5

41 "wonderful achievements . . .": Bryce, p. 128.

45 "The fates....": Weems, p. 138.

46 "beats the record...": Robert E. Peary, *Northward Over the Great Ice* (Frederick A. Stokes, 1898), vol. 2, p. 97.

47 "Will she always be...": Weems, p. 150.

Chapter 6

48 "I lay helpless...": Herbert, p. 115.

49 "We will all get home....": Weems, p. 164.

49 "He was gentle....": Weems, p. 168.

49 "I wonder if I am really going mad": Weems, p. 166.

50 "Peary was a very determined man....": Weems, p. 168.

53 "suspicious wooden feeling": Weems, p. 180.

53 "of no importance": Herbert, p, 121.

53 "an iron man . . .": Herbert, p. 139.

54 "too old for this kind of work": Weems, p. 199.

54 "Has the game been worth the candle?": Weems, p. 200.

55 "I shall never be quite the same again": Weems, p. 195.

Chapter 7

56 "I began to long....": Robert E. Peary, *The North Pole: Its Discovery in 1909 Under the Auspices of the Peary Arctic Club* (Frederick A. Stokes, 1910), p. 10.

60 "To me the final....": Weems, p. 227.

60 "Cook is an honorable man": Weems, p. 230.

61 "I believe in you, Peary": Weems, p. 236.

61 "I knew it was my last....": Peary, *The North Pole*, p. 10.

62 "Over the 89th!": Weems, p. 167.

62 "The Pole at last!!!....": Wally Herbert, "Did He Reach the Pole?" (*National Geographic Magazine*, September 1988), p. 388.

63 "The thing that was intended....": Weems, p. 273.

Chapter 8

65 "I pulled the thing off finally...": Weems, p. 284.

67 "within a stone's throw": Weems, p. 228.

68 "No one will ever know....": Weems, P. 325.

69 "Some credit for original discovery....": Bryce, p. 964.

69 "I knew it was my last game....": Peary, *The North Pole*, p.10.

70 "the restless wild essence of life": Weems, p. 34.

INDEX

Page numbers in **boldface** are illustrations.

Index